THANKSGIVING FUN

RONNE RANDALL

ILLUSTRATED BY ANNABEL SPENCELEY

Kingfisher

NEW YORK

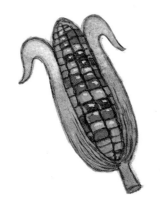

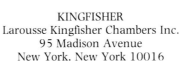

KINGFISHER
Larousse Kingfisher Chambers Inc.
95 Madison Avenue
New York, New York 10016

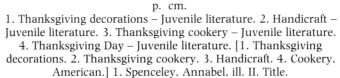

. First edition 1994
2 4 6 8 10 9 7 5 3 1
Copyright © Larousse plc 1994

Library-of-Congress Cataloging-in-Publication Data
Randall, Ronne.
Thanksgiving fun: great things to make and do/by Ronne Randall;
illustrated by Annabel Spenceley. – 1st American ed.
p. cm.
1. Thanksgiving decorations – Juvenile literature. 2. Handicraft –
Juvenile literature. 3. Thanksgiving cookery – Juvenile literature.
4. Thanksgiving Day – Juvenile literature. [1. Thanksgiving
decorations. 2. Thanksgiving cookery. 3. Handicraft. 4. Cookery,
American.] 1. Spenceley, Annabel, ill. II. Title.
TT900.T5R36 1994
745.594'1–dc20 93-48615 CIP

ISBN 1-85697-500-2

For permission to include copyright material, acknowledgment and
thanks are due to Greenwillow Books, William Morrow & Company Inc.
for "The First Thanksgiving" from *It's Thanksgiving* by Jack Prelutsky.

Edited by Abigail Willis
Designed by Brian Robertson

Printed in Spain

CONTENTS

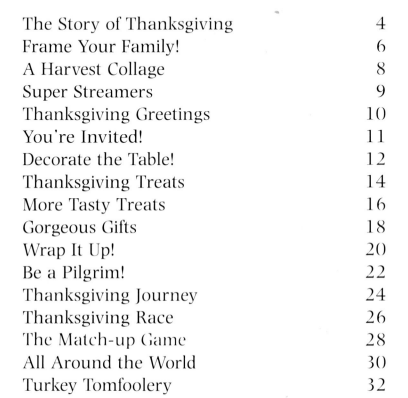

Welcome to **Thanksgiving Fun!** Inside this book you'll find a delightful assortment of activities to help you prepare for the Thanksgiving holiday. There are things to make for yourself and your friends, yummy recipes to try, games to play, and lots more. So get ready to have fun—and have a very happy Thanksgiving!

The Story of Thanksgiving

In December, 1620, a ship called the *Mayflower* landed in Plymouth Harbor, Massachusetts. On board were 102 Puritans. Calling themselves Pilgrims, they had come from England to seek religious freedom in the New World.

The Pilgrims faced great hardships in their first year. Food was scarce, and many died of hunger and disease. But the Native Americans helped them hunt and fish, and taught them to plant corn, pumpkins, and squash.

After their first harvest was gathered, the Pilgrims held a festival of Thanksgiving, with prayers, games, and a huge feast. They invited the Native Americans, who brought deer and turkeys.

In 1863, President Lincoln declared the last Thursday in November an official Thanksgiving holiday. Now, like the Pilgrims, we celebrate Thanksgiving with fun and feasting.

The First Thanksgiving

When the Pilgrims
first gathered together to share
with their Indian friends
in the mild autumn air,
they lifted their voices
in jubilant praise
for the bread on the table,
the berries and maize,
for field and for forest
for turkey and deer,
for the bountiful crops
they were blessed with that year.
They were thankful for these
as they feasted away,
and as they were thankful,
we're thankful today.

JACK PRELUTSKY

Frame Your Family!

Thanksgiving has always been a holiday to share with those we love. We celebrate the joy of being together, and give thanks for our families and friends.

Here's a wonderful gift you can make for your family, so that everyone remembers this Thanksgiving as an extra-special one. First, go out and gather some colorful autumn leaves. If they're not completely flat, you can put them between sheets of tissue or newspaper and press them between the pages of a heavy book. Next, find some family photos to copy, and draw or paint a family portrait. Don't forget to include yourself! Now, here's how to make a beautiful autumn-leaf frame for your portrait.

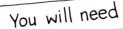

You will need

4 strips of heavy cardboard, about 2 inches wide
ruler
tape
scissors
glue
craft knife (an adult should help)
varnish

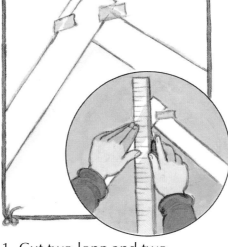

1. Cut two long and two short cardboard strips, to measure 2 inches longer than your picture. Tape them together at the corners.

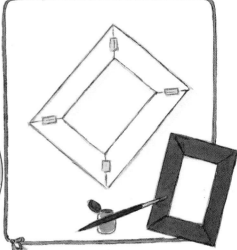

2. Neaten the corners by cutting diagonally and fitting them together. Secure with tape. Paint the frame a dark color.

MAPLE

OAK

HORSE
CHESTNUT

SUMAC

3. Glue the leaves to the cardboard and then varnish the frame. Tape your picture securely to the back of the frame.

4. To make a stand for the picture, cut out a cardboard wedge and tape it to the back of the frame.

A Harvest Collage

There are lots of ways you can help make your home look bright and festive for the Thanksgiving holiday. This fall collage, made from dried grass, leaves, cranberries, seeds, and beans, will look beautiful anywhere in the house!

You will need

cardboard

cranberries

dried beans

seeds (such as pumpkin and sunflower)

bark

leaves

dried grass

glue

1. If you like, give your collage a background color by painting the cardboard—but make sure the paint is dry before the next step!

2. Lightly sketch in your picture in pencil, and begin gluing your materials in place. Work in small areas, filling them in closely.

3. To make the apple tree shown here, you can use bark for the tree trunk, real leaves, and cranberries.

Try thinking up your own ideas for designs and materials to use. Look for interesting colors and textures—let your imagination take over!

These streamers are fun to make and look great in a window, above your bed, or even strung across the Thanksgiving table. To make the streamers really eye-catching, use bright fall colors. Take care when cutting around your turkey or leaf shape.

1. Fold a strip of crepe paper accordion-style. Make sure the sections are equal, and big enough for you to draw on.

2. On the top sheet, draw a simple turkey or leaf shape like the ones shown here. It must go all the way out to the edges.

3. Keeping the paper folded, cut around the shape. Be sure to leave some of each folded side uncut, or your streamer will fall apart.

Thanksgiving Greetings

It's fun to send greeting cards, especially when you've made them yourself. Your friends will love this card, with its pop-up surprise!

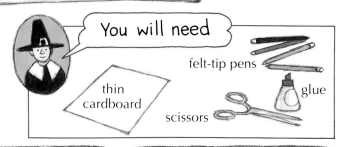

You will need

felt-tip pens

thin cardboard

scissors

glue

1. Cut out a large square from a sheet of thin cardboard. Fold in half, then in half again.

2. Use a ruler to draw a line across the folded corner to make a triangle. Fold toward the opposite corner.

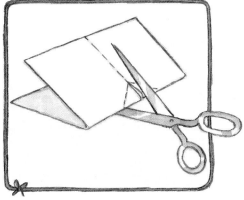

3. Open out and color the diamond shape red. Fold in half and cut along the center fold to the triangle tip.

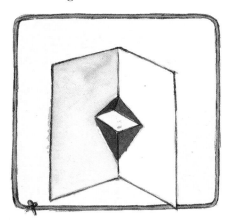

4. Fold the red part to make a beak, and tuck inside. Fold another cardboard square in half, and decorate.

5. Glue both pieces together. *Don't* glue the back of the beak! Finish the inside design and sign!

You're Invited!

Make your Thanksgiving Day guests feel really special by sending them these custom-made, stand-up invitations.

1. Fold a piece of cardboard in half, open out, and draw a Thanksgiving picture that extends over the top half.

2. Carefully cut around the outside of the picture on the top half only. (You may want to ask an adult to help.)

3. Write your invitation on the inside. When the card is folded, the picture will stand up!

Decorate the Table!

Here are some ideas to help give your Thanksgiving table a really festive look. Use brightly colored autumn leaves to make these lovely place mats and napkin rings. The cheerful turkey place cards will add a special finishing touch!

You will need

leaves

cardboard

glue

clear contact paper

aluminum foil

cardboard tube

paint

scissors

thin paper

felt-tip pens and crayons

Place Mats

1. Use one sheet of heavy cardboard for each mat. Glue on leaves in interesting patterns and different color combinations.

2. Using a sheet of contact paper 1½ inches larger overall than your mat, carefully cover the mat. Trim any excess paper.

Napkin Rings

For each napkin ring, you'll need a strip of foil 7 inches long by 3 inches wide.

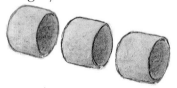

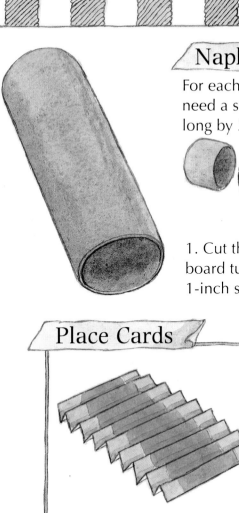

1. Cut the cardboard tube into 1-inch sections.

2. Wrap the foil around the ring and press firmly.

3. Where the foil ends overlap, glue on a small leaf.

Place Cards

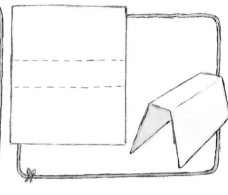

1. Use a sheet of thin paper about 5 x 11 inches. Paint as shown, then make narrow accordion folds.

2. Holding the folded strips flat, fold in half and glue together in the middle. Fan out the "tail feathers."

3. To make the card, fold a piece of thin cardboard (5 x 7 inches) in two places as shown.

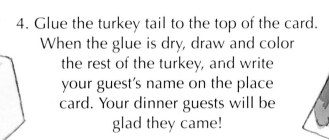

4. Glue the turkey tail to the top of the card. When the glue is dry, draw and color the rest of the turkey, and write your guest's name on the place card. Your dinner guests will be glad they came!

Thanksgiving Treats

One of the best things about Thanksgiving, of course, is eating! Here are some easy-to-fix, tempting treats you can make for the Thanksgiving dinner table, or for enjoying anytime over the Thanksgiving holiday.

Cranberry Punch

cranberry juice
ginger ale

apple juice
lemon slices

1. Make flavored ice cubes: dilute fruit juice or ginger ale with water.

2. Fill an ice cube tray and freeze. Put cubes into a large pitcher.

3. Pour equal amounts of juice and ginger ale into the pitcher.

4. Carefully cut some lemon slices to add to your punch.

Quick Cranberry Relish

2 cups of fresh cranberries
¼ cup orange juice
¼ cup water 1 cup sugar

1. Heat in a saucepan over a medium flame, stirring gently, for about 7–10 minutes until the cranberries pop open. Make sure an adult helps you use the stove.

2. Cool and serve with your Thanksgiving turkey. Yum!

Corny Cupcakes

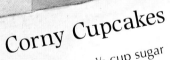

1 cup flour   ½ cup sugar
¼ cup soft butter   1 egg
¼ cup milk   1 tsp. salt
1 tsp. baking powder
Ready-made frosting
Candy corn to decorate

1. Ask an adult to preheat the oven to 375° F.

2. Sift the flour and sugar together into a mixing bowl.

3. Add the butter, milk, egg, sugar, salt, and baking powder. Beat until the mixture is smooth.

4. Pour into a muffin tin lined with cupcake liners. Put the tin into the oven for about 20 minutes.

5. When cool, spread frosting on top of the cupcakes and decorate with candy corn.

More Tasty Treats

Pumpkins have always been part of Thanksgiving, and no Thanksgiving dinner is complete without pumpkin pie for dessert. With this easy recipe, you can impress everyone with a scrumptious pumpkin pie you've made yourself! (But remember—don't use the oven without an adult's help.)

You will need

Pumpkin Pie

1 ready-made, unbaked 9-inch pie crust
2 large eggs
½ cup sugar
½ cup salt
1 tsp. cinnamon
½ tsp. ginger
¼ tsp. ground cloves or allspice
2 cups canned pumpkin
1½ cups evaporated milk or light cream

1. Ask an adult to preheat the oven to 450° F. Beat the eggs with the sugar, salt, and spices until they're well mixed.

2. Add the pumpkin and milk or cream, and mix well.

3. Pour the mixture into the pie crust and bake on the lower shelf of the oven for 10 minutes. Then lower the heat to 400° F.

4. Bake for another half-hour, or until done. To test, stick a knife into the center of the pie. If it comes out clean, the pie is ready!

Holiday Shapes

No one can resist these gingerbread cookies! Trace the shapes below onto thin paper, cut out, and trace onto cardboard. Then make the dough.

You will need

Ask an adult to preheat the oven to 375° F.

⅓ cup butter	1 small egg
¼ cup brown sugar	½ cup molasses
1 tsp. ginger	1½ cups flour
½ tsp. cinnamon	½ tsp. baking soda
¾ tsp. salt	¼ tsp. baking powder

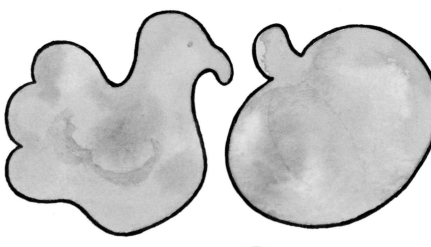

1. In a large mixing bowl, sift together the flour, baking soda, baking powder, spices, and salt.

2. Separately, mix together the butter, sugar, egg, and molasses. Combine with the first mixture and stir well. Chill for 2–4 hours.

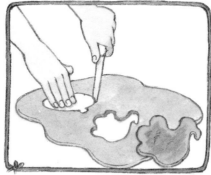

3. Roll out the dough onto a clean, floured surface until it's about 1/8 inch thick. Cut carefully around your cardboard patterns.

4. Place the cookies on a lightly greased baking sheet and bake for 8–10 minutes, until golden brown. Then cool, and enjoy!

Gorgeous Gifts

If you've been invited to Thanksgiving dinner, you might want to take a gift for your host or hostess. This Indian-corn wreath, with its warm fall colors, is a perfect Thanksgiving Day present to hang on the front door!

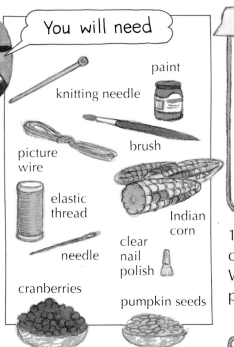

You will need

paint

knitting needle

brush

picture wire

elastic thread

Indian corn

needle

clear nail polish

cranberries

pumpkin seeds

Corn Wreath

1. Ask an adult to cut the corn into 2-inch sections. With the knitting needle, poke a hole through them.

2. Thread the corn onto the picture wire. Form a circle and fasten the ends. Decorate with dried flowers.

This bracelet and necklace set, made from pumpkin seeds and cranberries, is great for Thanksgiving giving!

Joyful Jewelry

1. Carefully paint the seeds in bright colors. When the paint is dry, seal it with a coat of clear nail polish.

2. Thread the seeds and cranberries alternately on lengths of elastic thread, then tie the ends securely.

Wrap It Up!

If you're giving gifts at Thanksgiving, you'll want to wrap them as attractively as possible. It's easy and fun to design and print your own wrapping paper—and it will make your gifts even more special! Here are some autumnal ideas for you to try, but you'll soon find yourself thinking up new Thanksgiving shapes and colors.

You will need

plain brown wrapping paper
poster paints
apples or potatoes
leaves
paintbrush
knife (see safety note)

Decide what colors you want to use for your prints, and pour some of each color into a separate saucer. The paint shouldn't be too thick—dilute with water if necessary.

To make turkey designs, dip your hand in paint and make hand prints all over the paper. Using your thumbprint as the turkey's neck and head, paint in eyes, beaks, and legs.

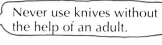

Never use knives without the help of an adult.

Safety Note

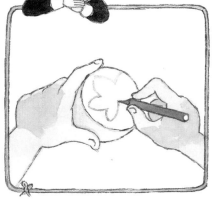

1. Cut an apple or potato in half. Lightly draw a simple shape onto the flat part of the fruit or vegetable.

2. Cut around the shape so it forms a raised surface. Dip it into paint and press firmly onto a large sheet of paper.

Leaf printing

Leaf prints in bright fall colors make especially pretty wrapping paper designs.

1. Collect leaves in as many different shapes, colors, and sizes as you can find.

2. Gently dip each leaf into the paint, making sure the paint is not mixed too thinly.

3. Press the leaf down firmly and lift up carefully.

Wrap your presents with ribbons to match your printed designs, and the packages will be as beautiful as the presents themselves!

Be a Pilgrim!

The Pilgrims believed in living pure and simple lives, and their clothing reflected their beliefs. Children and adults dressed alike, in plain and modest clothes of black, white, and gray. If you and your friends want to dress up like Pilgrims, here are some costume pieces you can make.

You will need

cardboard
construction paper
scissors
glue
pencil
belt

Pilgrim Hat

1. Cut the brim for your hat from a large piece of black cardboard. Make the inside circle just big enough to fit over your head.

2. Roll another piece of cardboard into a cone shape. The base of the cone should fit over the inside circle of the brim.

3. Carefully cut some small tabs all around the brim and tape or glue these to the inside of the cone so it is firmly fixed on.

4. Cut the top off the cone. Draw around the top of the hat onto cardboard and cut out a circle. Glue the circle securely in place.

5. Use a belt or construction paper in black and white, to make a band and buckle to complete your special pilgrim hat!

Pilgrim Collar

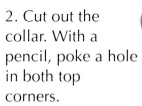

1. Draw a shape like the one shown, on white construction paper. The inside circle should fit around your neck.

2. Cut out the collar. With a pencil, poke a hole in both top corners.

3. Thread a piece of yarn through the holes, and tie securely with a bow when worn.

Pilgrim Bonnet

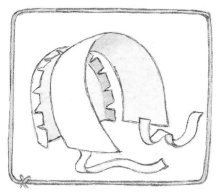

1. Cut a strip of white cardboard long enough to go over your head to your chin and wide enough to reach the back of your head.

2. Hold the curved strip against a piece of cardboard and trace the shape for the back of the bonnet. Draw a line ½ inch outside this.

3. Cut out along the outer line, and cut tabs to the inner line. Tape these to the inside of the bonnet front. Add yarn or ribbon ties.

Thanksgiving Journey

Thanksgiving is a day for sharing, and many people travel thousands of miles just to be with their families at this special time. This poem, written more than a hundred years ago, is about one family's journey.

Thanksgiving Day

Over the river and through the wood,
  To Grandfather's house we go;
    The horse knows the way
    To carry the sleigh
  Through the white and drifted snow.

Over the river and through the wood—
  Oh, how the wind does blow!
    It stings the toes
    And bites the nose
  As over the ground we go.

Over the river and through the wood,
  To have a first-rate play.
    Hear the bells ring,
    "Ting-a-ling-ding!"
  Hurrah for Thanksgiving Day!

Over the river and through the wood,
　Trot fast, my dapple-gray!
　　　Spring over the ground
　　　Like a hunting hound,
　For this is Thanksgiving Day!

Over the river and through the wood,
　And straight through the barnyard gate.
　　　We seem to go
　　　Extremely slow—
　It is so hard to wait!

Over the river and through the wood—
　Now Grandmother's cap I spy!
　　　Hurrah for the fun!
　　　Is the pudding done?
　Hurrah for the pumpkin pie!
　　　　　　　LYDIA MARIA CHILD

Thanksgiving Race

You will need

buttons of various colors (for counters)

die

Play this game to see how quickly you can get to Grandma and Grandpa's house! *To play:* Throw the die to see who goes first—the person who throws the highest number starts. If you land on a red or green space, follow the instructions. The first person to reach the house is the winner!

START

Bridge is down! Miss a turn.

Wind is at your back. Move ahead 2 spaces.

Take a shortcut. Move ahead 2 spaces.

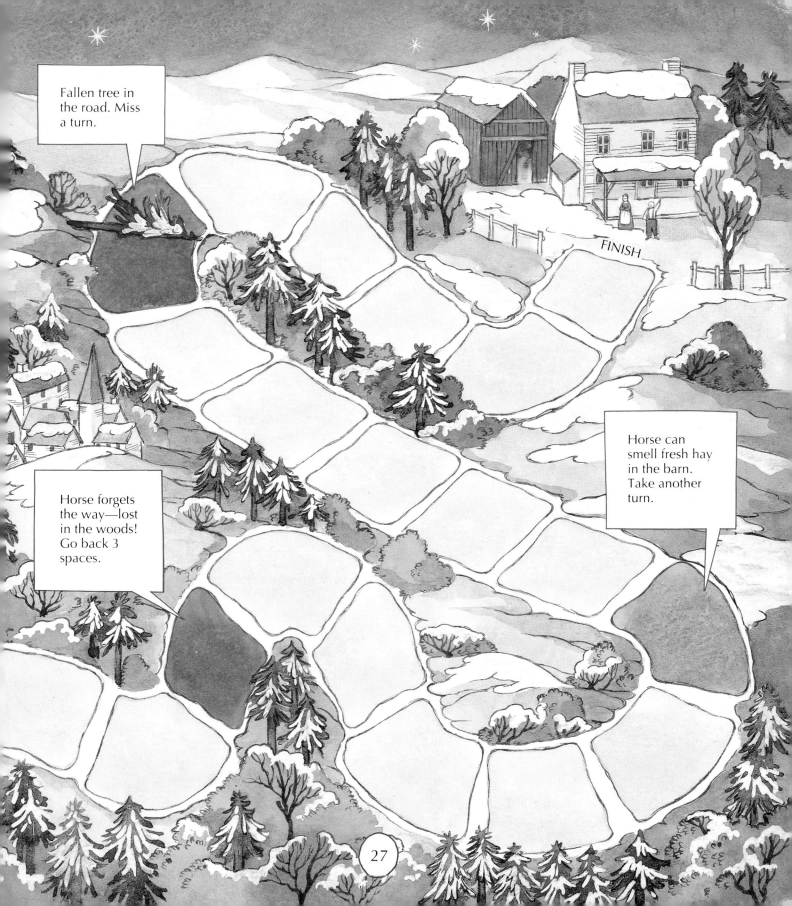

The Match-up Game

Here's an after-dinner game for two players. *To make the cards:* Draw 32 equal-sized rectangles on thin cardboard. Copy or trace each design four times, then color and cut out.

To play: Shuffle the deck and divide into two piles of 16. Together, turn over one card at a time. If the cards match, the first person to call out the name of the object keeps both cards. Keep playing until no cards are left. The person with the most cards wins!

You will need

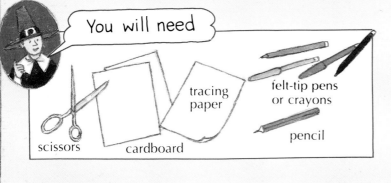

tracing paper

felt-tip pens or crayons

pencil

scissors   cardboard

Pumpkin!

MAYFLOWER

TURKEY

CORN

LEAF

PIE

PUMPKIN

HAT

ACORN

All Around the World

In Canada, Thanksgiving is celebrated just as it is in the United States, but on a different day—the second Monday in October. There are thanksgiving festivals in other parts of the world, too. Throughout history, people of every culture and religion have come together to give thanks at harvest time.

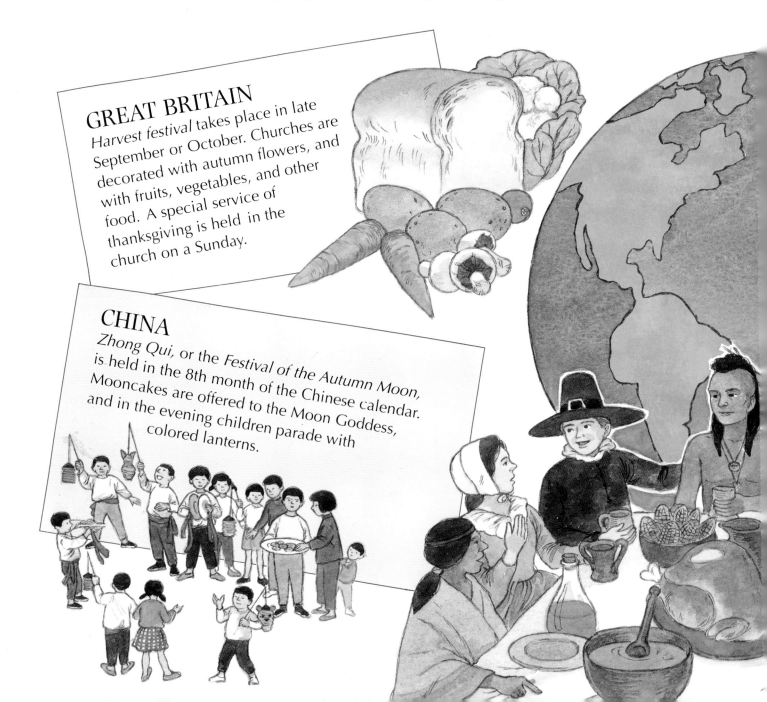

GREAT BRITAIN
Harvest festival takes place in late September or October. Churches are decorated with autumn flowers, and with fruits, vegetables, and other food. A special service of thanksgiving is held in the church on a Sunday.

CHINA
Zhong Qui, or the Festival of the Autumn Moon, is held in the 8th month of the Chinese calendar. Mooncakes are offered to the Moon Goddess, and in the evening children parade with colored lanterns.

JUDAISM WORLD-WIDE

The festival of *Sukkot* lasts for nine days. Jewish families build a temporary booth called a *sukka*, which is decorated with leaves, branches, and newly harvested fruits and vegetables. Prayers are said and meals are eaten in the *sukka*.

INDIA

The harvest festival of *Onam* is celebrated in the state of Kerala, in southern India. Homes are decorated with flowers, and food is distributed to the poor and needy. There are more festivities in the evening, including fireworks.

LITHUANIA

During harvest celebrations in this part of eastern Europe, the last sheaf of grain is dressed up with ribbons and flowers to make a doll called a *boba*, or "old woman." The *boba* is kept until spring, so that the spirit of the crop stays alive until replanting.

Turkey Tomfoolery

When is a Turkey scary?

When it's a-goblin'!

What language do turkeys speak?

Gobble-de-gook!

Why did the turkey cross the road?

To visit the chicken on the other side.

THANKSGIVING WORD CHALLENGE

How many words of 4 letters or more (not counting plurals) can you make from the letters in THANKSGIVING? There are at least 40—answers below. (No peeking!)

asking	king	shin	tank	visit
gain	knight	sigh	task	vista
gait	knit	sight	than	
gang	night	sing	thank	
gnat	saint	sink	thin	
hang	sang	skin	thing	
hank	sank	snag	think	
having	satin	stain	vain	
hint	saving	stink	vanish	
insight	shaving	tang	vast	